Hmong Learning *series*

let's learn Hmong together!

Other Books by Mai Nhia Yang

Baby Numbers

let's learn Hmong together!

mai nhia yang

Vang Publishing House

Cover Design: Mai Nhia Yang

First Edition
Published by Vang Publishing House

ISBN: 978-1-972879-13-9

Printed in United States of America

www.vangpublishinghouse.com

Dedication

This book is lovingly dedicated to the children and families who carry the beauty of the Hmong language and culture forward each day.

May these pages bring joy, connection, and pride as you learn, grow, and count together.

To every child discovering their voice, and to every parent, caregiver, and educator guiding them. This book is for you.

A Guide for Parents & Caregivers

Thank you for choosing this book to support your child's early learning journey.

Learning numbers is one of the first steps in building strong foundational skills in early childhood. In this book, children are introduced to numbers in both English and Hmong, helping to support language development while also strengthening cultural identity.

You can use this book in simple and meaningful ways:

• Read together
Point to each number and say it out loud in both languages.
Encourage your child to repeat after you.

• Count with objects
Use everyday items like toys, snacks, or steps to practice counting in real life.

• Take your time
Children learn best through repetition. It's okay to revisit the same page again and again.

• Make it interactive
Ask questions like, "Can you find three things?" or "Let's count together!"

• Celebrate effort
Learning a new language or strengthening one takes time. Celebrate every attempt and progress your child makes.

This book was created to be simple, engaging, and meaningful, so that learning feels natural and joyful.

There is one sun in the sky.

Muaj ib lub hnub nyob saum ntuj.

There are two friends at the park.

Muaj ob tug phooj ywg ua si tom tiaj.

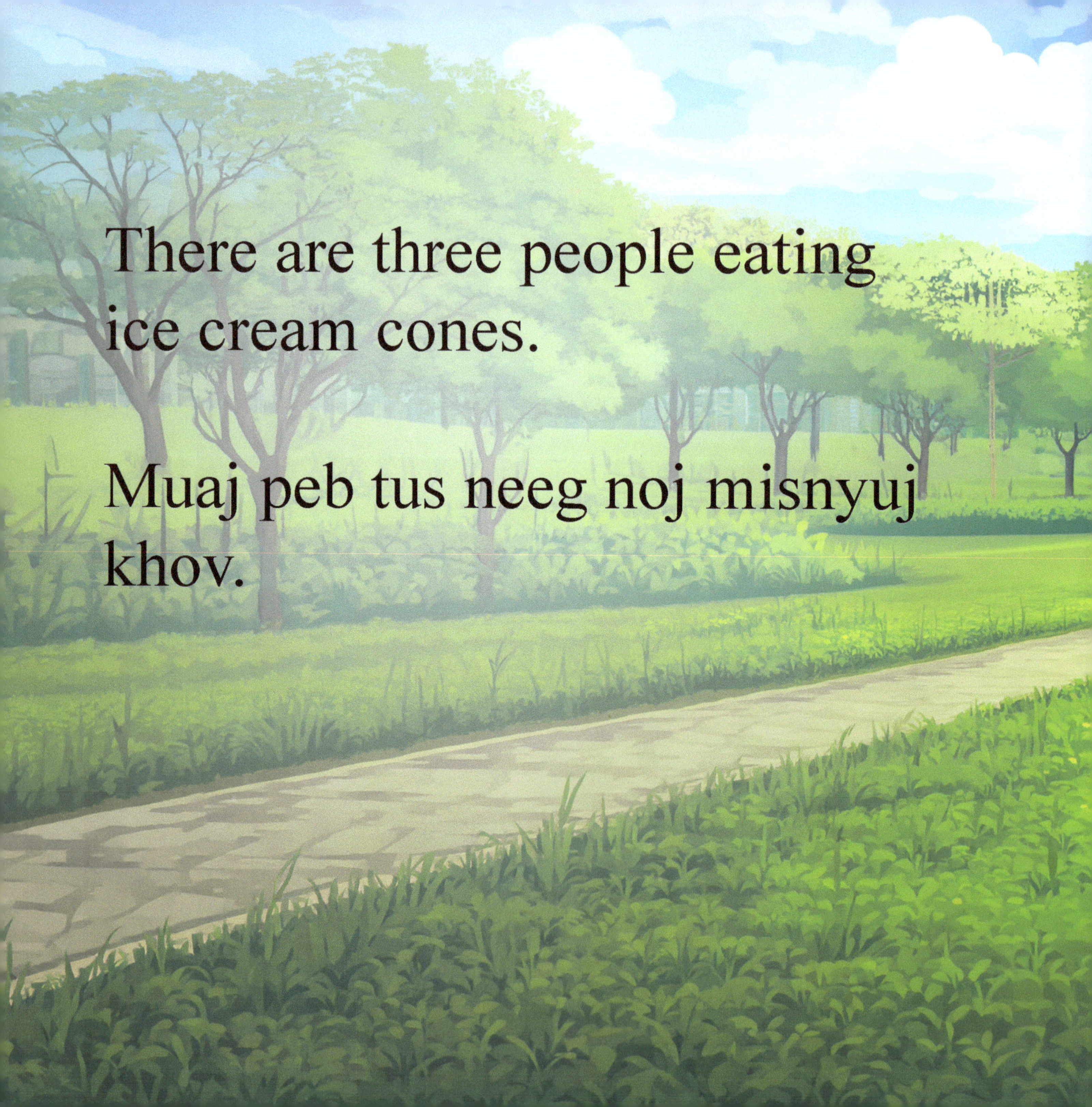

There are three people eating ice cream cones.

Muaj peb tus neeg noj misnyuj khov.

There are four cars in the parking lot.

Muaj plaub lub tsheb nyob hauv chaw nres tsheb.

There are five trees along the sidewalk.

Muaj tsib tsob ntoo nyob raws txoj kev taug kev.

There are six boats in the lake.

Muaj rau lub nkoj nyob hauv pas dej.

There are seven flowers in the field.

Muaj xya lub paj nyob hauv lub tshav.

There are eight candles on the table.

Muaj yim tus tswm ciab nyob saum rooj.

There are nine shining stars in the sky.

Muaj cuaj lub hnub qub ci ntsa iab saum ntuj.

There are ten books on the shelf.

Muaj kaum phau ntawv saum lub txee.

There are eleven lights on the street.

Muaj kaum ib lub teeb ntawm txoj kev.

There are twelve pictures hanging on the wall.

Muaj kaum ob daim duab dai saum phab ntsa.

There are thirteen chairs in the backyard.

Muaj kaum peb lub rooj zaum nyob tom qab tog tsev.

There are fourteen cans on the ground.

Muaj kaum plaub lub kaus poom nyob hauv av.

Sprite
fanta
Orange
Truly
HERD SELTZER

There are fifteen clothes hangers on the clothing rack.

Muaj kaum tsib tus pas khuam khaub ncaws saum lub txee dai khaub ncaws.

There are sixteen pairs of shoes by the door.

Muaj kaum rau nkawm khau nyob ntawm qhov rooj.

There are seventeen toys in the living room.

Muaj kaum xya tus khoom ua si nyob hauv lub chav nyob.

B
B
C

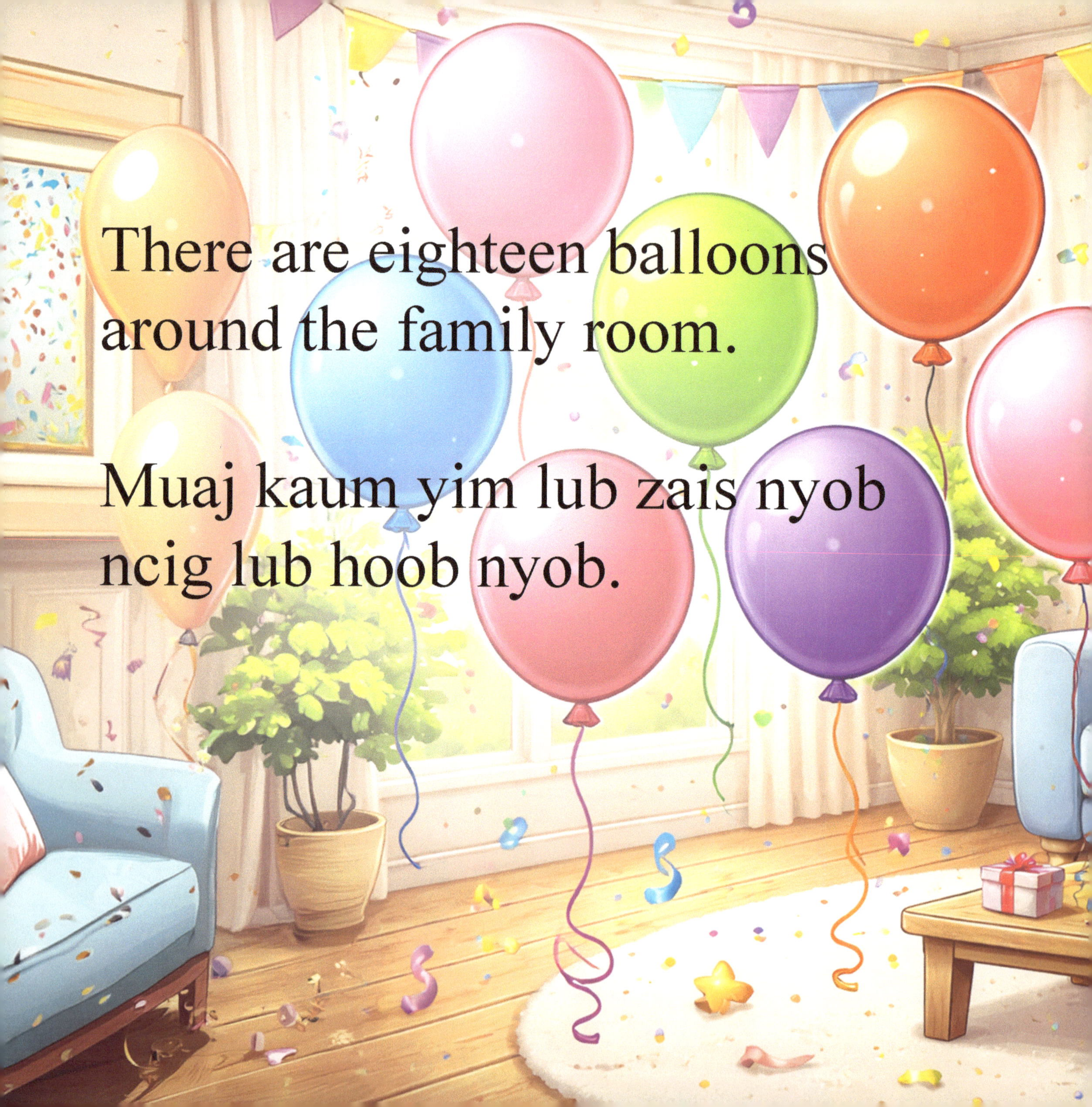

There are eighteen balloons around the family room.

Muaj kaum yim lub zais nyob ncig lub hoob nyob.

There are nineteen bean bag chairs in a pile.

Muaj kaum cuaj lub tog zaum uas yog cov hnab taum ua ib pawg.

There are twenty pairs of socks in the laundry room.

Muaj nees nkaum txais nkawm thom khwm hauv lub chav ntxhua khaub ncaws.

About the Author & Illustrator

Mai Nhia Yang is an early childhood educator with a deep passion for helping young children learn through culture, language, and play. Through her work, she strives to create meaningful learning experiences that support early development while honoring identity and heritage.

As both the author and illustrator of this book, Mai Nhia brings together education and creativity to make learning Hmong numbers engaging, simple, and joyful for children and families.

www.ingramcontent.com/pod-product-compliance
Lightning Source LLC
LaVergne TN
LVHW070151110826
845147LV00002B/369
9781972879139